Steck Vaughn

Level C

Language Exercises

Y0-CAZ-041

Betty Jones

Saranna Moeller

Cynthia T. Strauch

Harcourt Achieve

Rigby • Steck-Vaughn

www.HarcourtAchieve.com

1.800.531.5015

About the Authors

Saranna S. Moeller has been a teacher in the elementary grades for over twenty-five years. Moeller received her bachelor's degree in education from the University of Houston. She now operates the Refugio Learning Center in Texas.

Betty Jones earned her master's degree in education from Prairie View A & M University. Jones has been an elementary teacher for over twenty-five years.

Cynthia T. Strauch attained her master's degree in education at Texas A & I University. Strauch is also an experienced elementary school teacher, with over twenty-one years of service.

Acknowledgments

Illustrations: Laura Eisenhour, Holly Cooper, Mike Obershan, and Robin Borgers

Photography: P.3 John Katz; p.4 Rick Williams; p.27 NASA; p.29 National Park Service; p.34 Florida News Bureau Department of Commerce; p.36 © Cynthia Ellis; p.45 © Zoological Society of San Diego.

Macmillan/McGraw-Hill School Publishing Company: Pronunciation Key, reprinted with permission of the publisher, from *Macmillan School Dictionary 1*. Copyright © 1990 Macmillan Publishing Company, a division of Macmillan, Inc.

ISBN 0-7398-9115-4

© 2004 Harcourt Achieve Inc.

All rights reserved. No part of the material protected by this copyright may be reproduced or utilized in any form or by any means, in whole or in part, without permission in writing from the copyright owner. Requests for permission should be mailed to: Copyright Permissions, Harcourt Achieve Inc., PO Box 26015, Austin, Texas, 78755.

Rigby and Steck-Vaughn are trademarks of Harcourt Achieve Inc. registered in the United States of America and/or other jurisdictions.

3 4 5 6 7 8   054   11 10 09 08 07 06

Table of Contents

Unit 5 Composition

Unit 6 Study Skills

Final Reviews

Synonyms

> ■ A **synonym** is a word that means almost the same
> thing as another word.
>   EXAMPLE: small—little, jump—leap

■ **Write a synonym for each word shown under
the lines. Choose synonyms from the box.**

Many people have heard _____
                                    (tales)

about the Cyclops. He was a _____
                                         (large)

monster. He had a body like a _____.
                                            (human)

But his face was _____. He had only
                        (different)

one eye in the _____ of his forehead.
                      (center)

His _____ was a cave on an
            (house)

island. The people who lived near the island were

_____ of the Cyclops. He was
      (scared)

very mean and _____.
                        (loud)

afraid
huge
person
home
stories
unusual
middle
noisy

■ **Write a sentence using the synonyms <u>funny</u>
and <u>silly</u>. Tell about something you like.**

_____

_____

> ■ An **antonym** is a word that means the opposite of another word.
>   EXAMPLES: on—off, wet—dry

■ **Write an antonym for each word shown under the lines. Choose the antonyms from the box.**

| play   small   easy   long   fun   back |

A gerbil is a _____, furry
            (large)

animal. It has long _____ legs. Its
                    (front)

tail is _____ and hairy. A gerbil is
        (short)

_____ to care for, and it is a
(hard)

_____ pet. It loves to
(boring)

_____ .
(work)

■ **Write the sentences. Complete each one with an antonym for the underlined word.**

1. Do you think Ann will <u>win</u> or (lose, leave)?

_____

_____

2. Will he do a backbend <u>now</u> or (never, later)?

_____

_____

Lesson 3

Homonyms

> - A **homonym** is a word that sounds the same as another word but has a different spelling and a different meaning.
>
>   EXAMPLES: **they're, their, there**
>   Use <u>they're</u> to mean "they are."
>   **They're** playing now.
>   Use <u>their</u> to mean "belonging to them."
>   Did they bring **their** bats?
>   Use <u>there</u> to mean "in that place" or to help begin a thought.
>   He threw it **there. There** are two teams.

- **Write <u>they're</u>, <u>their</u>, or <u>there</u>.**

1. Lee and Vin raced down the street carrying

   _____ baseball gloves.

2. "All the players are _____ in the park," yelled Lee.

3. "I hope _____ ready for the big game today," said Vin.

4. All the players quickly took _____ places on the field.

5. "Look, _____ are people cheering for us!" cried Vin.

6. "I think _____ here to see us win the game," said Lee.

7. Vin and Lee's team won _____ game by one point.

- **Write a sentence about a ball game using <u>they're</u>, <u>their</u>, or <u>there</u>.**

_____

_____

- Remember that a homonym is a word that sounds the same as another word.

  EXAMPLES: **hear, here**   **to, two, too**

  Use <u>hear</u> to mean "to listen to."

  Did you **hear** that funny song?

  Use <u>here</u> to mean "in this place."

  The tapes are over **here.**

  Use <u>to</u> to mean "toward" or to go with words like <u>make</u> and <u>buy</u>.

  Juan rode his bike **to** the store. He wanted **to** buy a tape.

  Use <u>too</u> to mean "more than enough" or "also."

  The music is **too** loud. I like that song, **too.**

  Use <u>two</u> to mean "the number 2."

  Those **two** speakers sound very good.

- **Underline the correct homonym.**

1. Put the new speakers over (hear, here).

2. Listen (to, too, two) the soft music.

3. Do you (hear, here) the band play?

4. Those (to, too, two) compact discs were on sale.

5. Dad bought some tapes, (to, too, two).

6. We will dance when we (hear, here) the music.

7. Mom will come in (to, too, two) watch us.

8. (Here, Hear) comes Dad to show us a dance.

9. His (to, too, two) feet just float across the floor.

10. Do you (hear, here) us clapping for him?

- **Use <u>hear</u> and <u>here</u> in a sentence about music.**

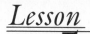
> ▪ Many words have more than one meaning.
>   EXAMPLE: <u>Pound</u> means "a weight equal to
>   16 ounces." Buy a **pound** of peanuts. <u>Pound</u> also
>   means "hit hard over and over." **Pound** the stake
>   into the ground.

▪ **Read the meanings on the right. Write the number
of the meaning for each underlined word.**

1. My little brother was playing with his

   spinning <u>top</u>. _____

2. Mom asked him to turn on the outside <u>light</u>. _____

3. The strong wind had turned over the <u>light</u>

   doghouse. _____

4. I heard the dog <u>bark</u> at the squirrel. _____

5. It was climbing up the <u>bark</u> of the tree. _____

6. The squirrel went to the <u>top</u> of the tree. _____

7. It was <u>light</u> enough to jump onto a thin

   branch. _____

8. But there wasn't enough <u>light</u> to see where the

   squirrel went next. _____

light
1. not heavy
2. something by
   which we see

bark
1. hard outside
   covering of
   a tree
2. the sound a
   dog makes

top
1. the highest
   part
2. a toy

▪ **Write a sentence using the first meaning of <u>light</u>.**

_____

_____

- A **prefix** is a word part added to the beginning of a base word to change the meaning of the word.
    EXAMPLES: The prefix <u>un</u>- means "not" or "the opposite of." The prefix <u>re</u>- means "again."
    un- + usual = **un**usual, meaning "not usual"
    re- + heat = **re**heat, meaning "heat again"

- **Add the prefix <u>un</u>- to the words below.**
  Then write the meaning of the new word.

  1. happy _____ _____

  2. fair _____ _____

  3. even _____ _____

  4. safe _____ _____

  5. tie _____ _____

- **Add the prefix <u>re</u>- to the words below.**
  Then write the meaning of the new word.

  1. open _____ _____

  2. test _____ _____

  3. use _____ _____

  4. read _____ _____

- **Write one sentence with a word that has the prefix <u>un</u>-.**
  Write one sentence with a word that has the prefix <u>re</u>-.

  1. _____

  2. _____

- A **suffix** is a word part added to the end of a base word to change the meaning of the word.

  EXAMPLES: The suffixes -er and -or mean "a person or thing that ___."

  heat + -er = heat**er,** meaning "a thing that heats"

  sail + -or = sail**or,** meaning "a person that sails"

- **Add the suffixes to the words to make new words.**

1. climb + er = _____

2. teach + er = _____

3. visit + or = _____

4. travel + er = _____

5. act + or = _____

6. mark + er = _____

7. paint + er = _____

8. sing + er = _____

- **Write each sentence with a new word made by adding -er to the word in ( ).**

1. The ___ clipped the roses.   (garden)

   _____

2. He cleaned his gloves in the ___.   (wash)

   _____

3. He and a ___ ate lunch.   (farm)

   _____

4. Then he hired a new ___ to help him.   (work)

   _____

5. The new worker used to be a ___.   (teach)

   _____

Compound Words

> ■ A **compound word** is made by joining one word
> with another word.
>   EXAMPLE: air + plane = airplane

■ **Write the compound word made by joining each
pair of words.**

1. birth + day =

_____

2. after + noon =

_____

3. skate + board =

_____

4. fire + place =

_____

5. cat + fish =

_____

6. rain + bow =

_____

7. snow + ball =

_____

8. sun + rise =

_____

9. water + fall =

_____

10. down + stairs =

_____

■ **Underline the compound word in each sentence.
Then write the two words that form the compound word.**

1. The birthday party is a surprise.   _____ _____

2. Is everyone here?   _____ _____

3. Let's run downstairs and hide!   _____ _____

4. Everything is ready.   _____ _____

5. The party is for a classmate.   _____ _____

6. I brought a football as a gift.   _____ _____

■ A **contraction** is a word made by joining two words. When the words are joined, a letter or letters are left out. An **apostrophe** (') shows where the missing letter or letters would be.

EXAMPLES: I + will = I'll, there + is = there's, is + not = isn't

■ **Rewrite the sentences. Use contractions in place of the underlined words.**

| doesn't | Here's | I'll | isn't | she'll | She's | There's |

1. She is going camping this weekend.

_____

2. I think she will go fishing in the lake.

_____

3. Inuk does not like to fish.

_____

4. Here is some fresh bait.

_____

5. There is enough for everyone to use.

_____

6. After we catch the fish, I will help cook them.

_____

7. It is not hard to do.

_____

■ **Write a sentence telling what you will do this weekend. Use the contraction I'll.**

_____

- **Write the synonym for each underlined word.**

  1. The <u>small</u> dog stars in a circus. (tiny, big) _____

  2. Sparky does some <u>simple</u> tricks. (hard, easy) _____

  3. He can <u>jump</u> high into the air. (crawl, leap) _____

  4. He stands on his <u>back</u> legs. (rear, front) _____

  5. Sparky <u>likes</u> doing his tricks. (hates, enjoys) _____

- **Write the antonym for each underlined word.**

  1. Is the clown act <u>first</u> or (never, last)? _____

  2. The clown is <u>happy</u>, but has a (sad, red) face. _____

  3. Her nose is <u>big</u>, but her ears are (small, flat). _____

  4. She has a <u>narrow</u> tie and (skinny, wide) shoes. _____

  5. Was the clown's wink <u>fast</u> or (quick, slow)? _____

- **Choose and underline the correct word in each sentence.**

  1. The dancing bear is over (here, hear).

  2. It likes dancing (too, to, two) the music.

  3. There are only (to, two, too) acts left.

  4. (They're, Their, There) about to begin.

  5. The stars take (they're, their, there) final bows.

  6. Darla has fun at the circus, (to, too, two).

  7. There are many things to see and (here, hear).

- **Write two sentences. Use a different meaning for <u>feet</u> in each sentence.**

    1. _____

    2. _____

- **Write two sentences. Use a different meaning for <u>match</u> in each sentence.**

    1. _____

    2. _____

- **Underline each word that begins with a prefix.**

    1. pack, unpack   4. relive, live   7. rename, name

    2. copy, recopy   5. make, remake   8. true, untrue

    3. untie, tie   6. take, retake   9. unsure, sure

- **Underline each word that ends with a suffix.**

    1. clean, cleaner   4. teacher, teach   7. heater, heat

    2. visitor, visit   5. dry, dryer   8. lead, leader

    3. work, worker   6. act, actor   9. sailor, sail

- **Underline each contraction. Circle each compound word.**

    1. There's the tightrope.   4. We can't see everything.

    2. We'll be inside the tent.   5. Let's eat something.

    3. The clown isn't in the airplane.   6. Doesn't everyone like the circus?

■ **Rewrite the letter. Use a homonym for the words in dark print. Use a contraction for the words that are underlined.**

> Dear Tom,
>   It was very hot **hear** in the house today. I went **too** the pool **too** cool off. My **to** friends, Anna and Rosa, were **their.** We <u>did</u> <u>not</u> do anything but swim. <u>We</u> <u>will</u> go back tomorrow. <u>I</u> **here** <u>it</u> <u>will</u> be even hotter then. <u>I</u> <u>will</u> be sure to tell Anna and Rosa to bring **they're** beach ball.

■ **Write a story about summer fun. Include these words in your story:**

1. a synonym of <u>bright</u>
2. an antonym of <u>cold</u>
3. the homonyms <u>pale</u>, <u>pail</u>

4. a compound word
5. a word with the prefix <u>re-</u> or <u>un-</u>
6. a word with the suffix <u>-er</u> or <u>-or</u>

_____

_____

_____

_____

_____

_____

_____

_____

_____

_____

_____

_____

_____

_____

_____

Lesson 10   Sentences

> ■ A **sentence** is a group of words that tells or asks something. It stands for a complete thought.
> EXAMPLE: Sally dreamed about the picnic.

■ **Underline the sentences.**

1. Eva and Sue ate fried chicken.

2. Smelled good to eat.

3. Did Sue find the rolls?

4. Sue and Eva?

5. Eva ran to get a swing.

6. Swung up to the stars.

7. Is Sue hungry again?

8. Potato salad.

■ **Match each group of words in A with a group of words in B to make a complete sentence. Write the sentences below.**

A	B
The ants	looking for crumbs.
They were	marched in a row.
Eva	saw them coming.
She moved	was for Eva, not the ants.
The food	her blanket right away.

1. _____

2. _____

3. _____

4. _____

5. _____

> ▪ Remember that a sentence is a group of words that tells or asks something. It stands for a complete thought.

▪ **Choose the sentence in each pair of word groups below. Write the sentence.**

1. Catherine saw Superdog. A most unusual dog.

   _____

2. Flew high as a rocket. Superdog flew high.

   _____

3. Where is Superdog? Superdog with his trainer?

   _____

4. Superdog read about the dog show. The big show.

   _____

5. Went to the show. Superdog went to the show.

   _____

6. Win a ribbon? Did he win a blue ribbon?

   _____

7. Superdog won "Best of Show." "Best of Show."

   _____

▪ **Read the paragraph below. Draw a line through each group of words that is not a sentence.**

Catherine and Superdog walked to the dog show. What did Superdog do there? Surprised all the judges. The judges in the chairs. Superdog ran as fast as a train. Jumped over a tall building in a single bound.

- Some sentences are **statements.** They tell something.
  EXAMPLE: Hawaii is a beautiful state.
- Some sentences are **questions.** They ask something.
  EXAMPLE: Is Hawaii a beautiful state?

- **Write S in front of each statement.**
  Write Q in front of each question.

_____ 1. Hawaii has many miles of beaches.

_____ 2. Does Hawaii have over a hundred islands?

_____ 3. The sun shines there on most days.

_____ 4. Many kinds of flowers grow in Hawaii.

_____ 5. Do farmers grow pineapples?

_____ 6. Sugarcane is an important crop in Hawaii.

_____ 7. Hawaii is called the Aloha State.

_____ 8. "Aloha" is a Hawaiian greeting.

_____ 9. Would you like to go to Hawaii?

_____ 10. When do you want to go?

- **Copy the sentences below. Underline the**
  statement once. Underline the question twice.

  Many people visit Hawaii to ride the waves. Which beach
  do they like best?

_____

_____

_____

> - Some sentences are **commands.** They tell somebody to do something.
>   EXAMPLE: Squeeze all the juice out of the lemons.
> - Some sentences are **exclamations.** They show strong feelings or surprise.
>   EXAMPLE: What a sour taste that lemon has!

- **Write C in front of each command. Write E in front of each exclamation.**

_____ **1.** How delicious those strawberries look!

_____ **2.** Slice the bananas.

_____ **3.** Add the water to the mix.

_____ **4.** What a great lunch we'll have outside!

_____ **5.** Clean the grill well.

_____ **6.** How golden that chicken is!

_____ **7.** Pass the salad, please.

_____ **8.** The ants got the cake!

_____ **9.** What a good idea this picnic was!

- **Write a sentence that is a command. Tell somebody to do the first step in making your favorite food.**

_____

- **Write a sentence that is an exclamation. Write what you would say after eating something good.**

_____

- A sentence has two parts. One part is called the **subject.** The subject tells who or what the sentence is about.   EXAMPLE: **The snow** is deep.

- **Underline the subject in each sentence.**

1. We went sledding today.

2. The sled flew down the hill.

3. Jamie threw a snowball.

4. Kamal lost his hat.

5. Skaters were on the pond.

6. The ice was smooth.

7. Alan liked to spin around.

8. He went very fast.

9. The girls slid by us.

10. A red glove was in the snow.

- **Complete each sentence by adding a subject.**

1. _____ put on her ice skates.

2. _____ helped his little sister.

3. _____ sat on the sled.

4. _____ went down the hill.

5. _____ was very cold.

6. _____ watched the snow fall.

7. _____ liked the snow.

8. _____ makes tracks in the snow.

9. _____ are on the ice.

10. _____ can skate well.

11. _____ turned to the left.

12. _____ went home.

Predicates in Sentences

> ■ A sentence has two parts. One part is called the subject. The other part is called the **predicate.** The predicate tells what the subject is, was, or does.
> EXAMPLE: That big zoo **is nearby.**

■ **Underline the predicate in each sentence.**

1. The cub growled at the bird.
2. The huge ape swung from a bar.
3. Barry liked the camels.
4. These tiny snakes are harmless.
5. Monkeys are fun to watch.

6. Vic petted the sheep.
7. A calf was in the yard.
8. Lee saw the baby ducks.
9. The pigs cooled off.
10. An owl hooted softly.

■ **Complete each sentence by adding a predicate.**

1. The clucking chickens _____.

2. The baby goats _____.

3. Barbara _____.

4. All the elephants _____.

5. A zookeeper _____.

6. The bears _____.

7. Those tigers _____.

8. Many people _____.

9. A sleeping bat _____.

10. The balloon man _____.

11. Everyone _____.

Combining Subjects and Predicates

> • Two short sentences with the same predicate can be **combined** to make a new sentence. The two parts are joined by and.   EXAMPLE: Lou laughed. + Gina laughed. → Lou **and** Gina laughed.
>
> • Two short sentences with the same subject can be combined to make a new sentence. The two parts are joined by and.   EXAMPLE: Fred counted his coins. + Fred paid for the tickets. → Fred counted his coins **and** paid for the tickets.

• **Combine the sentences. Write the new sentence.**

1. Mom went on the ride. Trish went on the ride.

   _____

2. Bob stood in line. The boys stood in line.

   _____

3. Lee ate lunch. Jung ate lunch.

   _____

4. Donna took a picture. Donna sat down to rest.

   _____

5. Ed popped the balloons. Ed won a prize.

   _____

6. Linda went to the petting zoo. Linda fed the animals.

   _____

   _____

7. Ryan saw the bears. Ryan rode on the train.

   _____

Lesson 17

Combining Sentences

- Two short sentences that closely share an idea can be combined to make one sentence.
- The two sentences may be joined with connecting words such as <u>or</u>, <u>and</u>, or <u>but</u>. A comma is placed before these words.

  EXAMPLES: Tony found shells. + Amy caught seaweed. →

  Tony found shells, **and** Amy caught seaweed.

  I can't swim. + I can wade. →

  I can't swim, **but** I can wade.

  Fish from here. + Go to the dock. →

  Fish from here, **or** go to the dock.

- **Underline the two short sentences that were combined to make each sentence.**

  1. The wind howled, and the sand blew around.

  2. The children can swim, or they can play ball.

  3. The water is cold, but the sand is warm.

  4. The sea is blue, and the foam is white.

  5. Dad carried our lunch, and we carried the chairs.

- **Combine the sentences using the word in ( ). Write the new sentence.**

  1. Take your pail. Fill it with sand.   (and)

  _____

  2. You can make a castle. You can make a cave.   (or)

  _____

  3. We can't play on rocks. We can play on sand.   (but)

  _____

> ■ If a sentence tells about more than one main idea,
> it should be rewritten as two sentences.
>   EXAMPLE: Most plants have seeds, some seeds
>   are good to eat. → Most plants have seeds.
>   Some seeds are good to eat.

■ **Read the sentences. Write two sentences
for each.**

1. The seeds must be planted, this is done
   in many ways.

   _____

   _____

2. A seed floated in the breeze, it was
   very windy.

   _____

   _____

3. You can eat these seeds, Shameka will
   gather some more.

   _____

   _____

4. Birds and animals eat seeds, you can buy
   seeds for them in a store.

   _____

   _____

- **For each pair, underline the group of words that is a sentence.**

  1. Owls have large eyes. Catch food at night.

  2. Whales are. They live in the ocean.

  3. Lizards are reptiles. Are cold-blooded.

  4. What do chipmunks? Do you like chipmunks?

- **Write S in front of the statement. Write Q in front of the question.**

  _____ 1. Why did the kitten buy a fan?

  _____ 2. It wanted to be a cool cat.

  _____ 3. How did the heater make the dog feel?

  _____ 4. The heater made it feel like a hot dog.

- **Write C in front of the command. Write E in front of the exclamation.**

  _____ 1. Give the cat its food.

  _____ 2. What beautiful fur your cat has!

  _____ 3. Don't let the cat go outside.

  _____ 4. Your cat is so playful!

- **Underline the subject. Circle the predicate.**

  1. The cat washed its face with its paw.

  2. Kirk threw a ball of yarn to the cat.

  3. The cat took a long nap.

  4. Kirk fed the cat after its nap.

- **Combine the sentences to make a new sentence.**

   1. Erin fed her mouse. Erin cleaned its cage.

   _____

   _____

   2. Raul held the mouse. Ann held the mouse.

   _____

   _____

   3. The mouse feels warm. Its nose feels cool.

   _____

   _____

- **Read the sentences. Write two sentences for each.**

   1. My friend comes over, my dad takes us to see a movie.

   _____

   _____

   2. We stand in line, we get our tickets.

   _____

   _____

   3. We find a place to sit, we share some popcorn.

   _____

   _____

   4. The theater gets dark, the movie begins.

   _____

   _____

- **Rewrite the story below, but make it less choppy. Combine each pair of sentences that is underlined. When you are finished, you will have six sentences in all.**

The sea horse is an amazing animal! It is only about five inches tall. It is covered with bony plates. The sea horse swims by using the fin on its back. It is not a strong swimmer. Ocean currents carry it. They move the sea horse from one place to another. The sea horse can easily stop itself. It just wraps its tail around a sea plant.

_____

_____

_____

_____

_____

_____

_____

_____

_____

- **Write a story about another animal that lives in the sea. Use at least two statements, one question, and one exclamation.**

_____

_____

_____

_____

_____

_____

_____

- **Imagine you are a diver. Write a story about the things you saw when you were diving in the ocean. Use at least two statements, one question, and one exclamation.**

_____

_____

_____

_____

_____

_____

Lesson
19

Nouns

> ■ A **noun** is a word that names a person, place, or thing. The words <u>a</u>, <u>an</u>, and <u>the</u> are clues that show a noun is near.
>   EXAMPLES: a pilot, the moon, the island

■ **Underline the two nouns in each sentence.**

1. The astronaut looked out the window.

2. Clouds circled the earth.

3. The ocean looked like a lake.

4. Another astronaut ate her lunch.

5. An apple floated inside the cabin.

6. One man put on his spacesuit.

7. The astronaut walked in space.

8. The newspaper had pictures of him.

■ **Write a noun from the list to complete each sentence.**

best	ocean	radio
cheer	happy	ship
day	hear	tall
doctor	over	the

1. They landed in the _____.

2. A _____ sailed over to them.

3. The _____ checked their health.

4. The news was on the _____.

5. We all yelled out a _____.

6. It was an exciting _____.

Lesson
20
Singular and Plural Nouns

> - A **singular noun** names one person, place, or thing.
>   EXAMPLES: bee, fox, bench
> - A **plural noun** names more than one person, place, or thing. Add -s to most nouns to change them to mean more than one. Add -es to nouns that end with s, sh, ch, x, or z to change them to mean more than one.
>   EXAMPLES: bees, foxes, benches

- **Make the nouns plural.**

1. skate _____

2. car _____

3. parade _____

4. toe _____

5. brush _____

6. class _____

7. inch _____

8. box _____

9. dish _____

10. dollar _____

11. leash _____

12. watch _____

- **Rewrite each sentence. Choose the correct noun in ( ).**

1. The fish are in a new (tank, tanks).

    _____

2. All the (plant, plants) are fresh.

    _____

3. Use that (net, nets) to catch the fish.

    _____

4. Both those (boy, boys) visit the fish store.

    _____

> - A **proper noun** names a particular person, place, or thing. It begins with a capital letter.
>   EXAMPLES: Bill Clinton, Seattle, Park School
> - A **common noun** does not name a particular person, place, or thing.
>   EXAMPLES: president, city, school

- **Write C for a common noun. Write P for a proper noun.**

_____ **1.** girl

_____ **2.** Mexico

_____ **3.** mountain

_____ **4.** country

_____ **5.** Alabama

_____ **6.** Tolman Company

_____ **7.** lake

_____ **8.** Helen Keller

_____ **9.** Friday

_____ **10.** Mojave Desert

_____ **11.** building

_____ **12.** doctor

- **Read the sentences. Draw one line under the common noun. Circle the proper noun.**

1. The <u>ocean</u> was very rough on (Tuesday.)

2. The waves pounded Sand Beach.

3. The beach is in Mexico.

4. Some boys were there from Portland.

5. Julio spied a seaplane.

6. Another boy saw a Flying Eagle.

7. The plane was flying to Canada.

8. Sarah waved to the pilot.

■ A **verb** usually shows action. It tells what a person, place, or thing is or was doing.
EXAMPLES: The cub **sleeps** in the shade.
A tiger **ran** across the field.

■ **Underline the verb in each sentence.**

1. A beautiful bird chattered in the forest.
2. Elephants drank from the stream.
3. An animal leaped in the air.
4. Meg read this in a book about Africa.
5. She got it from the library.

■ **Choose a verb from the list to complete each sentence.**

| buzz | grow | roar | search | swing |

1. We _____ for butterflies.
2. Many plants _____ by the stream.
3. Monkeys _____ from branches.
4. The insects _____ above us.
5. The lions _____ loudly.

■ **Use an action verb in a sentence about animals in Africa.**

_____

_____

Verbs in the Present

> - Verbs can show that an action happens in the **present.**   EXAMPLE: The game **starts** now.
> - Verbs in the present used with singular subjects, except I and you, end in -s.   EXAMPLES: Troy **likes** to pitch. I **like** to pitch.
> - Verbs in the present used with plural subjects have no special endings.   EXAMPLE: The girls **play** kickball.

■ **Complete each sentence with the correct verb.**

1. The bell _____ at 10:00.   (ring, rings)

2. The children _____ outside to play.   (run, runs)

3. Gabriela _____ to Jenny. (wave, waves)

4. The students _____ to their friends.   (talk, talks)

5. The new girl _____ at the ball.   (swing, swings)

6. My teacher _____ us laugh.   (make, makes)

7. Claudia _____ a joke.   (tell, tells)

8. The boys _____ for the game.   (plan, plans)

■ **Write sentences with verbs in the present.**

1. Tell what you do during recess at school.

_____

_____

2. Tell what other people do during recess.

_____

_____

> ■ Verbs can show that an action happened in the
> **past.** Add the endings -d or -ed to most verbs to
> show that something happened in the past.
> EXAMPLE: Yesterday we **washed** our bikes.

■ **Underline the verb in each sentence. Write P in**
front of each sentence with a verb in the past.

_____ 1. My friends like to ride to the park.

_____ 2. The wheels turned around and around.

_____ 3. They stopped at the light.

_____ 4. I squeezed the black handlebars.

_____ 5. We pedal as far as we can.

_____ 6. They rested for a half hour.

■ **Rewrite the sentences. Change each verb from**
the present to the past by adding -d or -ed.

1. We enter the bike race.

   _____

2. We start the race together.

   _____

3. We walk our bikes up the hill.

   _____

4. The dogs chase our wheels.

   _____

5. I hope to win.

   _____

> ■ A **linking verb** does not show action. It links, or joins, the subject to a word in the predicate. Verbs such as <u>am</u>, <u>is</u>, <u>are</u>, <u>was</u>, and <u>were</u> are linking verbs.
> EXAMPLES: Those insects **are** crickets.
> They **were** noisy.

■ **Write <u>L</u> in front of each sentence that has a linking verb.**

_____ 1. The crickets are loud tonight.

_____ 2. They chirp in the grass.

_____ 3. The dogs bark at the cars.

_____ 4. They were quiet earlier.

_____ 5. An owl screeches in the tree.

_____ 6. It is afraid of the dogs.

_____ 7. The white cat meows at her kitten.

_____ 8. She tells it not to wander.

_____ 9. The birds are asleep in their nests.

_____ 10. A jet roars over the house.

_____ 11. Everyone is quiet inside.

_____ 12. Just listen to the sounds at night!

■ **Use a linking verb in a sentence that tells about another sound you can hear at night.**

_____

> - Use <u>am</u> with the word I.
>   EXAMPLE: I **am** ready to go fishing.
> - Use <u>is</u> with one person, place, or thing.
>   EXAMPLE: Joe **is** ready to go, too.
> - Use <u>are</u> with more than one and with the word <u>you</u>.
>   EXAMPLES: We **are** all ready now.
>   **Are** you ready to go?

- **Write <u>am</u>, <u>is</u>, or <u>are</u>.**

The children _____ fishing. Joe _____ the first

to catch a fish.

He says, "It _____ too small. I will put it back into

the water. When I _____ a few years older, I might

catch it again!"

"You _____ smart," says Mary. "It _____ good

to throw fish back when they are too small."

"I _____ sure I have something big!" shouts Sam.

Mary and Joe help Sam pull the fish into the boat.

"That _____ not a fish," says Mary. She holds up

an old tin can. "People spoil our fishing spot with junk. I

_____ ready to put up a 'No Dumping' sign here."

"Two signs _____ here now," says Sam. "They

_____ over there behind that pile of junk!"

Using *Was* and *Were*

> - Use <u>was</u> and <u>were</u> to tell about the past.
> - Use <u>was</u> with one person, place, or thing.
>   EXAMPLE: Chris **was** busy in the kitchen.
> - Use <u>were</u> with more than one and with the word <u>you</u>.
>   EXAMPLES: The dishes **were** in the sink.
>   We **were** glad that you **were** here to help.

- **Write <u>was</u> or <u>were</u>.**

1. Ben _____ making a house for his dog.

2. He _____ working on it in the garage.

3. The boards _____ too long.

4. The saw _____ sharp.

5. Ben _____ using a saw to cut the boards.

6. Then he _____ looking for the nails.

7. Where _____ the nails?

8. They _____ behind the boards.

9. Ben _____ careful when he used the hammer.

10. Then all the boards _____ nailed in place.

11. Ben _____ ready to paint the doghouse.

12. Blue _____ his favorite color.

13. Ben hoped that blue _____ his dog's favorite color, too.

14. Ben and his dog _____ excited about the new doghouse.

Helping Verbs

> ▪ A **helping verb** helps the main verb. <u>Have</u>, <u>has</u>, or
> <u>had</u> helps a main verb show action in the past.
>   EXAMPLES: Rita has moved to a cottage.
>   They have packed their bags.
>   The farmer had milked the goat.

▪ **Underline the helping verb. Circle the main verb.**

1. The sun has risen.

2. The rooster had remembered to crow.

3. The cows have chewed their grass.

4. The girls had collected the eggs.

5. Dad has baked some fresh bread.

6. We have eaten breakfast.

▪ **Rewrite the sentences using the correct verb in ( ).**

1. I (has, have) walked to the park.

_____

2. A gentle rain (has, have) started.

_____

3. It (has, had) rained yesterday.

_____

4. Pat (has, had) picked out an umbrella last week.

_____

> - Use <u>does</u> with a singular subject to show the present.
>   EXAMPLE: Anna **does** all the costumes.
> - Use <u>do</u> with I, <u>you</u>, and plural subjects to show the present.
>   EXAMPLE: Alan and Lyn **do** want to see the play.
> - Use <u>did</u> without a helping verb to show the past.
>   EXAMPLE: Ed **did** a play about pets.
> - Use <u>done</u> with a helping verb to show the past.
>   EXAMPLE: Jenna has **done** her part.

- **Underline the correct verb.**

1. Our class (done, did) a play.

2. We had (done, did) one act.

3. Jo (does, do) well at acting.

4. Bob had (did, done) the costumes.

5. We all (does, do) a silly dance.

6. I (do, does) like to dance.

> - Use <u>sees</u> with a singular subject to show the present.
>   EXAMPLE: Anna **sees** a runner.
> - Use <u>see</u> with I, <u>you</u>, and plural subjects to show the present.
>   EXAMPLE: Alan and Lyn **see** the first runners.
> - Use <u>saw</u> without a helping verb to show the past.
>   EXAMPLE: Ed **saw** the high jump contest.
> - Use <u>seen</u> with a helping verb to show the past.
>   EXAMPLE: Jenna has **seen** a lot of track meets.

- **Underline the correct verb.**

1. We (saw, seen) a track meet today.

2. Mom said, "I (see, sees) our seats."

3. We (saw, seen) the high jump contest.

4. Di (sees, see) the last winner.

5. We all shouted, "I (see, sees) the prizes!"

6. The runners had (seen, saw) the crowd.

- Use <u>gives</u> with a singular subject to show the present.
  - EXAMPLE: Anna **gives** the actors a gift.
- Use <u>give</u> with I, <u>you</u>, and plural subjects to show the present.
  - EXAMPLE: Alan and Lyn **give** helpful tips to the actors.
- Use <u>gave</u> without a helping verb to show the past.
  - EXAMPLE: Ed **gave** a speech before the play.
- Use <u>given</u> with a helping verb to show the past.
  - EXAMPLE: Jenna had **given** a speech last year.

Underline the correct verb.

1. They (give, gives) the play.
2. Kim (give, gives) a lot of help.
3. Our coach (gave, given) a speech.
4. He has (gave, given) it already.
5. Jim had (gave, given) a speech.
6. Our teacher (gives, give) prizes.
7. We have (gave, given) her flowers.
8. The crowd (gave, given) a cheer.

- Use <u>goes</u> with a singular subject to show the present.
  - EXAMPLE: Anna **goes** to the zoo.
- Use <u>go</u> with I, <u>you</u>, and plural subjects to show the present.
  - EXAMPLE: Alan and Lyn **go** to the zoo often.
- Use <u>went</u> without a helping verb to show the past.
  - EXAMPLE: Ed **went** to the children's zoo.
- Use <u>gone</u> with a helping verb to show the past.
  - EXAMPLE: Jenna has **gone** with Ed.

Underline the correct verb.

1. We (go, goes) to the zoo.
2. Sue (go, goes) with her family.
3. I have (gone, went) there before.
4. Our class (go, goes) this week.
5. Ann and Jill (go, goes) together.
6. Tim (went, gone) last year.
7. We (go, goes) in the spring.
8. You (gone, went) with us.

> - A **pronoun** is a word that takes the place of a noun.
> - Pronouns that take the place of singular nouns are
>   I, me, you, he, him, she, her, and it.
>   EXAMPLE: **Dave** ate slowly. **He** ate slowly.
> - Pronouns that take the place of plural nouns are
>   we, us, you, they, and them.
>   EXAMPLE: The popcorn is for **the boys**.
>   The popcorn is for **them**.

- **Choose the correct pronoun in ( ) to take the place of the underlined noun. Then rewrite the sentences.**

  1. Mrs. Cantu made popcorn for the class.   (She, They)

     _____

  2. Children love to eat popcorn.   (She, They)

     _____

  3. Hot air tosses popcorn around.   (it, them)

     _____

  4. Roger put salt on his popcorn.   (He, They)

     _____

  5. Don gave some popcorn to Colleen.   (her, them)

     _____

  6. Sue gave bowls to Bill and Bob.   (it, them)

     _____

- **Write two sentences using pronouns.**

  1. _____

  2. _____

> - Use these pronouns as **subjects**: I, you, he, she, it, we, and they. EXAMPLE: **I** like tall tales.
> - Use these pronouns as **objects** that follow an action verb: me, you, him, her, it, us, and them.
>   EXAMPLE: Paul Bunyan amazed **them.**

- **Write S if the underlined pronoun is used as a subject. Write O if it is used as an object.**

_____ 1. Davy Crockett beat him in a race.

_____ 2. We read about Mike Fink.

_____ 3. She told the tale in a whisper.

_____ 4. Pecos Bill kept them guessing.

_____ 5. It was a real adventure.

_____ 6. The blue ox surprised us.

- **Rewrite the sentences using a pronoun from the box in place of the underlined words.**

He	them	us	We

1. Jesse and I went to the rodeo.

_____

2. The friendly cowgirl roped two calves.

_____

3. The man couldn't believe her strength.

_____

4. The cowgirl gave Jesse and me a smile when she won.

_____

> ■ A **possessive pronoun** is a pronoun that shows who or what owns something. The pronouns my, our, your, his, her, its, and their are possessive pronouns.
>
> EXAMPLE: Janet rode **her** bike to school.

■ **Underline the possessive pronoun in each sentence.**

1. Two monkeys did tricks for their trainers.

2. My family watched the monkeys.

3. Their names were Peg and Mike.

4. Peg tried to eat our lunch.

5. Then she put on her hat.

6. Mike clapped his hands.

■ **Write the correct possessive pronoun in each blank.**

1. Bill lives in a house. _____ house is white.

2. I live in an apartment. _____ apartment has two bedrooms.

3. Sarah lives on a farm. _____ farm is very big.

4. During the summer, Tom and Donna live on a houseboat.

   _____ houseboat goes up and down the river.

5. My family has one car. _____ car is old.

6. You have a new bike. _____ bike is blue and white.

7. The tree is big. _____ branches are long and thick.

8. Brian has a little brother. _____ brother's name is Robert.

> - Use I in the subject of a sentence.
>   EXAMPLE: **I** took Sara skating.
> - Use me in the predicate of a sentence.
>   EXAMPLE: Bev was waiting for **me.**
> - Use I or me last when naming yourself and others.
>   EXAMPLES: Juana and **I** like skating.
>   Bev saw Carlos and **me.**

- **Complete the sentences with the words in ( ).**
  Be sure to put the words in the correct order.

1. _____ and _____ wanted to go skating. (Liz, I)

2. Some of our friends were waiting for _____ and

   _____. (me, her)

3. Sally went with _____ and _____ . (me, Liz)

4. _____ and _____ had a great time. (Liz, I)

5. _____ and _____ helped our friend Karen
   learn to skate. (I, Sally)

6. _____ and _____ held Karen's arms until she got
   to the rail. (I, Sally)

7. Karen smiled at _____ and _____ . (me, Sally)

8. Then _____ and _____ gave Karen a little push
   to get her started. (I, Sally)

9. Karen thanked _____ and _____ for helping her
   learn to skate. (me, Sally)

10. _____ and _____ were happy about that!
    (I, Sally)

Lesson 35

Adjectives

> ■ An **adjective** is a word that describes a noun or a pronoun. It tells which one, how many, or what kind.
> EXAMPLE: The **two** clocks made a **loud** ring.

■ **Underline the adjectives.**

1. The bright sunlight peeked through the window.

2. The noisy alarm woke me up.

3. It was a great day for the carnival.

4. I threw on my old clothes.

5. Three friends met me at school.

6. Funny clowns walked in the yard.

■ **Complete the sentences with adjectives from the list.**

big	empty	little	top
brown	first	muddy	white
cold	gold	new	clean
deep	happy	red	old

1. Ron won a _____ bear and a _____ cat.

2. Ann won a _____ tank with _____ fish in it.

3. The _____ girl chose a prize on the _____ shelf.

4. A balloon had a _____ bird and a _____ dog on it.

Unit 3, Grammar and Usage

43

Lesson 36

Comparing with Adjectives

> - Add -er to most adjectives to compare two persons, places, or things.
>   EXAMPLE: The rabbit was **smaller** than the hat.
> - Add -est to most adjectives to compare more than two persons, places, or things.
>   EXAMPLE: That is the **smallest** rabbit I've seen.

- **Underline the correct form of the adjective in each sentence.**

1. The magician's show was (longer, longest) than the clown's.

2. The clown's shoes were the (funnier, funniest) of all the shoes.

3. The stage was the (bigger, biggest) one I've ever seen.

4. Our laughs were the (louder, loudest) in the crowd.

5. Our seats were the (closer, closest) to the stage.

6. The tightrope was (higher, highest) than a building.

- **Add -er or -est to the underlined adjective. Write the new words.**

1. The hand is <u>quick</u> than the eye. _____

2. That magician is the <u>great</u> in the world. _____

3. This is the <u>proud</u> moment of his life. _____

4. The white bird is <u>light</u> than the rabbit. _____

5. The rabbit is <u>soft</u> than the bird. _____

6. That trick is <u>old</u> than this country. _____

> - Use a before words that begin with a consonant sound.   EXAMPLES: a child, a fresh egg
> - Use an before words that begin with a vowel sound.   EXAMPLES: an adult, an old egg

- **Write a or an.**

1. _____ barn

2. _____ apple

3. _____ doctor

4. _____ test

5. _____ adventure

6. _____ balloon

7. _____ animal

8. _____ bedroom

9. _____ door

10. _____ house

11. _____ old barn

12. _____ red apple

13. _____ good doctor

14. _____ easy test

15. _____ happy adventure

16. _____ orange balloon

17. _____ clown's act

18. _____ upstairs room

19. _____ open door

20. _____ old house

- **Write a or an to complete this poem.**

The elephant didn't see—

_____ cat,

_____ ostrich,

_____ owl,

or a lion!

It saw another elephant!

▪ An **adverb** is a word that describes a verb. It tells how, when, or where. Many adverbs end in -ly.

EXAMPLES: The pig walked **slowly. How?**
The pig walked **today. When?**
The pig walked **there. Where?**

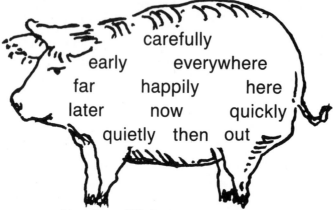

carefully
early   everywhere
far   happily   here
later   now   quickly
quietly   then   out

▪ **The words above are adverbs. Write each word under a heading below to show if the word tells how, when, or where.**

HOW?	WHEN?	WHERE?
_____	_____	_____
_____	_____	_____
_____	_____	_____
_____	_____	_____

▪ **Underline each adverb. Write how, when, or where.**

1. Shawn eats breakfast early. _____

2. Andy walked quietly. _____

3. We will eat later. _____

4. The bird flew there. _____

- Use the adjective <u>good</u> to mean "better than average."
  EXAMPLE: We had a **good** time.
- Use the adverb <u>well</u> to mean "in a good way."
  EXAMPLE: No one slept very **well.**

- **Write <u>good</u> or <u>well</u>.**

1. We saw a _____ movie at the sleepover.

2. Carmen danced very _____.

3. Everyone had a _____ time.

4. Lisa knows how to bake quite _____.

5. She made a _____ pizza for us.

- **Use <u>good</u> or <u>well</u> correctly in these paragraphs.**

Ben did not have a _____ time when he was ill.

But the doctor did his job _____, so soon Ben

was able to go outside. He went to a _____ beach

to surf.

His _____ friend Marty went with him. Marty could

surf very _____. They ran into the water and

waited for a _____ wave. It was a _____

day for surfing.

Ben and Marty get along _____ and always

have a _____ time together.

- **Underline the singular nouns. Circle the plural nouns.**

  1. The garden will be full of flowers.   **3.** The roses are in the sun.

  2. The children will mow the yard.   **4.** The birds love the birdbath.

- **Underline the common nouns. Circle the proper nouns.**

  1. Greg bought seeds at Plant World.   **3.** He waters his plants every Monday.

  2. Greg scattered the seeds.   **4.** He'll have corn in July.

- **Underline the action verb. Circle the linking verbs. Write <u>present</u> or <u>past</u> on the lines.**

  1. The daisies grow quickly.   _____

  2. The roses were droopy.   _____

  3. The pansies are colorful.   _____

- **Underline the correct verb.**

  1. A bee (rests, rest) in a flower.

  2. I (am, is, are) happy about the garden.

  3. It (were, was) raining yesterday.

  4. I (sees, see, seen) some new flowers.

  5. A garden (do, done, does) take time to grow.

  6. I (gone, goes, go) to the garden every day.

- **Underline the correct helping verb.**

  1. The family (has, have) moved.

  2. Dad (have, has) started his new job.

  3. The children (has, have) made some new friends.

- **Underline the correct pronoun.**

  1. (She, Her) took a break.

  2. This is (her, she) sandwich.

  3. Mary and (I, me) climbed a tree.

  4. We were in (we, our) yard.

  5. It is (me, my) birthday.

  6. Did you invite (their, them) to the party?

- **Underline each adjective that compares.**

  1. This leaf is the darkest on the twig.

  2. The twig is shorter than the branch.

  3. Can you reach the lowest branch?

  4. Your dog is older than my dog.

  5. My dog is faster than your dog.

  6. Our dogs are the greatest in the world.

- **Underline the adverbs.**

  1. The carrots grew quickly.

  2. The rain is falling softly.

  3. We'll have blossoms soon.

  4. The sun shines brightly.

  5. Winter came early this year.

  6. The soil is very rich.

- **Write <u>good</u> or <u>well</u>.**

  1. Dan slept _____.

  2. He ate a _____ breakfast.

  3. Dan has studied _____.

  4. He did _____ on his test.

  5. He got a _____ grade.

  6. Dan had a _____ day.

- **The underlined words in the paragraph below are wrong. Rewrite the paragraph correctly.**

Monster Mack is looking at himself in the mirror. Her hair look like dry grass. It need to be cut. Our brown eyes flash and sparkles in the bright light. The smile on his face are like a half moon. It disappear when you see his nose. His nose is smallest than his ears. It are good that her ears are huge, though. Them get everyone's attention when he wiggle they.

_____

_____

_____

_____

_____

_____

_____

_____

_____

_____

_____

- Write a funny paragraph describing another monster.
  Then go back and circle two singular or plural
  nouns, two common or proper nouns, an action
  verb, a helping verb, two pronouns, three adjectives,
  and two adverbs. If you don't have all of these,
  add them to your paragraph.

_____

_____

_____

_____

_____

_____

_____

_____

_____

_____

_____

_____

_____

_____

_____

_____

_____

> - Use a **capital letter** to begin proper nouns, such as days of the week, months, or holidays.
>   EXAMPLES: Monday, Friday, February, May, Thanksgiving, Canada Day
> - Use a **small letter** to begin the name of each season.
>   EXAMPLES: spring, summer, fall, winter

- **Rewrite the words. Use capital letters where they are needed.**

1. mother's day _____

2. winter _____

3. july _____

4. saturday _____

5. june _____

6. spring _____

7. thursday _____

8. april _____

- **Rewrite the sentences. Use capital letters where they are needed.**

1. This winter I am going to a parade on new year's day.

_____

_____

2. The parade is in january.

_____

3. It is on saturday.

_____

4. Last summer I went to a parade on labor day.

_____

_____

> - Use a capital letter to begin each word in proper nouns, such as names of people, family names, and place names.
>   EXAMPLES: Gary Woodlawn, Grandma Cary, London, Vermont
> - Use a small letter to begin a family name that comes after words like <u>my</u>, <u>your</u>, and <u>their</u>.
>   EXAMPLES: their uncle, my grandma

■ **Rewrite the words. Use capital letters where they are needed.**

1. uncle brian _____

2. new york _____

3. jamie smith _____

4. my grandfather _____

5. dallas _____

6. florida _____

7. aunt sue _____

8. charles _____

9. france _____

10. montreal _____

■ **Rewrite the sentences. Use capital letters where they are needed.**

1. We put on a play about ramona quimby.

_____

2. Did your uncle from san diego see it?

_____

3. I think aunt sarah liked it.

_____

4. susan allen had the part of ramona.

_____

> ■ Use a capital letter to begin the first word of a
> sentence.   EXAMPLE: The pony licked her hand.

■ **Write the sentences. Use a capital letter to begin
each sentence.**

1. would you like to have a pony?

_____

2. elena has a pretty red pony.

_____

3. her pony's name is Rosie.

_____

4. she rides her pony every day.

_____

5. it is tiny, but fast.

_____

6. the pony races through the fields.

_____

7. elena brushes her pony.

_____

8. then it takes a nap.

_____

9. a pony is a fun pet.

_____

> - Use a **period** (.) at the end of a sentence that tells something.
>   EXAMPLE: Ron has a new guppy**.**
> - Use a **question mark** (**?**) at the end of a sentence that asks a question.
>   EXAMPLE: Did he name it**?**
> - Use an **exclamation point** (**!**) at the end of a sentence that shows strong feelings.
>   EXAMPLE: What a good swimmer it is**!**

- **Use a period, question mark, or exclamation point at the end of each sentence.**

1. Guppies can live in a large bowl of water
2. Does the water need to be cleaned
3. Look at the pretty colors
4. Can you count how many there are
5. What a long tail that guppy has

- **Write the sentences. End each one with a period, question mark, or exclamation point.**

1. Do you feed guppies dry food

   _____

2. I can't believe how well they swim

   _____

3. The biggest guppy is named Butch

   _____

4. What is the little one's name

   _____

5. I like him the best

   _____

- An **abbreviation** is the shortened form of a word.
- Use a capital letter to begin an abbreviation for a title of respect or an abbreviation for the name of a place. Use a period at the end of these abbreviations.
  EXAMPLES: Ms., Mrs., Mr., Dr., Yellow Brick Rd.
- An **initial** is the first letter of a name. Capitalize an initial and put a period after it.
  EXAMPLE: M. C. Livingston for Molly Coe Livingston

- **Write the names. Correct the initials and the abbreviations that are underlined. Use capital letters and periods where they are needed.**

1. Laura i Wilder _____

2. mrs Tolan _____

3. Cherry Tree rd _____

4. dr Doolittle _____

5. a a Milne _____

6. ms t Lowry _____

7. Quimby st _____

8. mrs Banks _____

9. e m Thomas _____

- **Circle the mistakes in the sentence below. Write each correction on a line.**

ms Binney is in a book by b Cleary.

1. _____   2. _____

> - Use capital letters to begin abbreviations for days of the week. Use periods at the end of the abbreviations.
>   EXAMPLES: Sun., Mon., Wed., Thurs., Sat.
> - Use capital letters to begin abbreviations for months of the year. Use periods at the end of the abbreviations.
>   EXAMPLES: Jan., Feb., Apr., Aug., Nov., Dec.

- **Write the abbreviations for the days and the months. Use capital letters and periods where they are needed.**

1. Thursday _____

2. August _____

3. Sunday _____

4. March _____

5. Tuesday _____

6. February _____

7. Monday _____

8. September _____

9. October _____

10. Saturday _____

11. December _____

12. Wednesday _____

13. November _____

14. Friday _____

15. January _____

16. April _____

- **Circle the mistakes in the sentences below. Write each correction on a line.**

1. Lee asked me to a party on sat, sept 4th.

   _____   _____

2. I'm having a party on fri, oct 31st.

   _____   _____

> - Use a **comma** (,) after the words <u>yes</u> and <u>no</u> if they begin a sentence.   EXAMPLES: Yes, I saw the clowns at the parade. No, I didn't see them dance.
> - Use a comma to separate three or more items listed together in a sentence.   EXAMPLE: The float was red, white, and blue.

- **Write the sentences. Use commas where they are needed.**

1. Yes the band was in the parade.

_____

2. Patty Carlos and Jo rode on a float.

_____

3. We saw the bands clowns and floats.

_____

4. Horses fire engines and flags came next.

_____

5. No I didn't stay until the end.

_____

6. Yes I wanted to stay.

_____

7. We bought juice nuts and fruit to eat.

_____

8. Yes I waved to the woman on the horse.

_____

9. No she didn't see me.

_____

> - Use a comma between numbers for the day and year in the **heading** of a letter.   EXAMPLE: June 26, 2004
> - Use a comma between the city and state in an **address.**   EXAMPLE: Carbondale, Illinois 62901
> - Use a capital letter to begin the first word and all names in the **greeting** of a letter. Use a comma at the end of the greeting.   EXAMPLE: Dear Mom,
> - Use a capital letter to begin only the first word in the **closing** of a letter. Use a comma at the end of the closing.   EXAMPLE: Very truly yours,

- **Circle the words that should be capitalized in the letter. Add commas where needed.**

> 34 High Rise Street
> New York New York 10011
> April 3 2004
>
>
> dear gina
>
>   I'm really glad you got to come for a visit. I had a lot of fun. Please write soon.
>
>   your friend
>
>   Danielle

- **Rewrite these parts of a letter. Use capital letters and commas where they are needed.**

1. May 7 2004 _____

2. Miami Florida 33137 _____

3. dear alicia _____   **4.** with love _____

Using Apostrophes to Show Ownership

- Add an **apostrophe** (') and -s ('s) to nouns like <u>girl</u> to show that one person owns something.
  EXAMPLE: the **girl's** present
- Add an apostrophe after nouns like <u>girls</u> to show that more than one person owns something.
  EXAMPLE: the **girls'** presents
- Add an apostrophe and -s ('s) to plural nouns like <u>children</u> to show that more than one person owns something.   EXAMPLE: the **children's** presents

- **Rewrite each phrase to show ownership. Add an apostrophe or an apostrophe and -s to the underlined words.**

1. the <u>pilot</u> hat

_____

2. the <u>woman</u> car

_____

3. five <u>dogs</u> bones

_____

4. a <u>kittens</u> toys

_____

5. a <u>clown</u> hat

_____

6. many <u>mens</u> hats

_____

7. the <u>women</u> cars

_____

8. a <u>snowman</u> nose

_____

9. ten <u>kites</u> strings

_____

10. the <u>birds</u> nests

_____

- **Write a sentence telling about something that belongs to a friend or friends. Use an apostrophe or an apostrophe and -s to show who owns it.**

_____

_____

Lesson
49
Using Apostrophes in Contractions
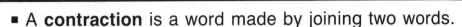

> - A **contraction** is a word made by joining two words.
> - Use an apostrophe to show that letters are left out.
>   EXAMPLES: **it's** = it is   **hasn't** = has not

- **Write contractions for the pairs of words.**
  Leave out the letters that are underlined.

  1. she + is _____

  2. we + are _____

  3. you + will _____

  4. I + have _____

  5. he + would _____

  6. she + has _____

- **Write contractions for the pairs of words.**

  1. has + not _____

  2. is + not _____

  3. were + not _____

  4. I + will _____

  5. that + is _____

  6. would + not _____

  7. they + will _____

  8. there + is _____

- **Rewrite the sentences. Use contractions for the**
  words that are underlined.

  1. Jay has not seen the movie.

  _____

  2. It is about a strange land.

  _____

  3. One year winter does not come.

  _____

  4. The people do not mind.

  _____

- Use **quotation marks** (" ") before and after the words a speaker says.   EXAMPLE: Mother said, "I'm going to leave for about an hour."
- Use a comma between the words the speaker says and the rest of the sentence. Put the comma before the quotation marks. Capitalize the first word the speaker says.   EXAMPLES: "We're leaving now," said Mother. **or** Mother said, "We're leaving now."

- **Read the cartoon. Think about who is talking and what they are saying.**

- **Answer the questions about the cartoon. Use quotation marks and commas where needed.**

   1. What did Carl say first?

   "Yes, I will," said Carl. **or** Carl said, "Yes, I will."

   2. What did Jane say first?

   _____

   3. What did Jane say about the butter?

   _____

   4. What was the last thing Carl said?

   _____

- **Correct the sentences. Circle letters that should be capitalized. Put periods, question marks, exclamation points, and commas where they are needed.**

1. mr and mrs kamp lived in a house on may street

2. one saturday the family cleaned the attic

3. ellen found an old letter from dr r m wilson

4. the letter came all the way from japan

5. we found a picture of roses daisies and tulips

6. did dad take that photo on valentine's day

7. no my aunt took the photo last april

8. what a mess the attic is

9. yes mom will clean out the attic next spring

10. ellen jason and beth will help mom

- **Rewrite the abbreviations. Use capital letters and periods where needed.**

1. tues _____

2. fri _____

3. mrs _____

4. elm st _____

5. dec _____

6. m c lee _____

7. apr _____

8. j r adams _____

9. feb _____

10. mon _____

11. smith rd _____

12. mr _____

13. sat _____

14. dr a roberts _____

15. ms n lincoln _____

16. aug _____

- **Add commas to these parts of a letter. Circle the small letters that should be capital letters.**

1. birmingham alabama 35205

2. august 18 2004

3. dear kim

4. yours truly

5. dear mom

6. austin texas 78759

7. sincerely

8. dear dr. west

9. your friend

10. dec. 1 2004

11. glendora california 91741

12. with love

- **Add apostrophes, quotation marks, and commas to these sentences where they are needed.**

1. This is Ellens game said Louisa.

2. Tom said Its her favorite.

3. Id like to play said Mike.

4. Mike Louisa and Nancy sat down to play.

5. It isnt hard to play Tom said.

6. Lets read the rules together said Louisa.

7. The games rules are printed on the box said Mike.

8. Were ready to begin playing said Louisa.

9. Mike said Ill go first.

10. Its Nancys turn to go first said Louisa.

11. Nancy doesnt want to play.

12. Shed rather read Ellens book.

■ Correct the story. As you read it, circle letters
that should be capitals. Put periods, question
marks, exclamation points, commas, apostrophes,
and quotation marks where they are needed.
Rewrite the title and the story on the lines.

<u>A Hidden Surprise</u>

jills cat is named sam_____ what a big smart

beautiful cat he is_____ one summer day, jill couldnt

find him_____ do you know where he was_____

he was under the porch with three new kittens_____

jill said your name is samantha now_____

_____

_____

_____

_____

_____

_____

_____

_____

_____

■ **Write a letter to Jill. Tell her what you think about her surprise. Use your address and today's date in the heading. Write a greeting and a closing. Be sure to use an abbreviation and a contraction in your letter. Use capital letters, periods, question marks, exclamation points, commas, and apostrophes. Check your letter for any mistakes.**

_____

_____

_____

_____

_____

_____

_____

_____

_____

_____

_____

_____

_____

- A **sentence** must tell a complete thought.
- Remember to begin a sentence with a capital letter and end it with a period, a question mark, or an exclamation point.
  - EXAMPLE: **Thought:** making our puppets
  - **Sentence:** We are making puppets.

- **Write each of these thoughts about making a puppet as a sentence.**

1. finding some yarn for our puppet's hair

_____

2. cutting yarn for the puppet's hair

_____

3. gluing the yarn to our puppet's head

_____

4. making a face on the puppet's head

_____

5. making a costume for our puppet

_____

6. sewing buttons on the costume

_____

7. dressing the puppet

_____

8. putting shoes on the puppet

_____

9. using the puppet in a puppet show

_____

- A **paragraph** is a group of sentences about one main idea. **Indent** the first line. To indent a paragraph, leave a space before the first word.
- A paragraph should have sentences about the same subject.

    EXAMPLE:

    Last night my brother and I put on a puppet show. We invited our parents and our little sister, Becky. Dad made popcorn, and everyone laughed.

- **Read the paragraph. Then write another paragraph. Tell what else you think happened in this puppet show. Be sure to indent.**

    My brother's puppet was named Morris. My puppet was Garfield. Morris was a fussy cat, and Garfield was his funny friend. Morris wouldn't eat much. Garfield loved to eat. Garfield asked my family to share their popcorn with him. Everyone agreed to share.

_____

_____

_____

_____

_____

_____

_____

Writing Topic Sentences

- A **topic sentence** tells the main idea, or topic, of a paragraph.
- All sentences in a paragraph should be about that topic.
  EXAMPLE: Liquid soap bottles make wonderful hand puppets. Just turn the bottle upside down, and paint a face on the bottom part. If you wish, glue a piece of cloth around the middle of the bottle. Stick your finger in the top of the bottle. There's your puppet!

- **Underline the topic sentence in each paragraph.**

Many people are needed to put on a puppet show. Someone must make the puppets and the set. Others must move the puppets and act in the show. Someone is needed to seat people and dim the lights.

_____

Shadow puppets are different from other kinds of puppets. You look at the shadow of the puppet instead of the puppet. The puppets are held and moved in front of a light so their shadows look alive.

_____

The person holding the puppet makes the puppet move. Some puppets move by strings that can be pulled. Others fit over a hand and move when the hand moves. Some puppets seem to talk when they are held the right way.

- **Details** after the topic sentence in a paragraph should tell more about the main idea.

  EXAMPLE: Liquid soap bottles make wonderful hand puppets. Just turn the bottle upside down, and paint a face on the bottom part. If you wish, glue a piece of cloth around the middle of the bottle. Stick your finger in the top of the bottle. There's your puppet!

- **Circle the topic sentence. Underline the four sentences that give details about the main idea. Write the circled and underlined sentences in a new paragraph.**

Our puppet show was a great success. Parents, friends, and neighbors came to see it. I am going to learn how to swim this summer. Altogether, we sold twenty tickets and made $10.00. Rita already knows how to swim. Everyone liked the show and clapped for about two minutes after it was over. My uncle's name is Tony. He knows how to swim well. A good time was had by all!

_____

_____

_____

_____

_____

- The details in a paragraph can be arranged in different ways. One way to arrange details is to put them in the **order** in which they happen.
- Words such as <u>first</u>, <u>next</u>, <u>then</u>, and <u>finally</u> help to show order.

   EXAMPLE: To make a ball-and-pencil puppet, **first** punch a sharp pencil into a soft ball. **Next,** wrap a piece of cloth just under the ball. **Then** tie a ribbon around the top part of the cloth. **Finally,** glue yarn hair on the ball and draw a face with markers.

- **Write numbers to show the right order in the paragraphs.**

_____ Next, give the people a program that lists the puppet characters. _____ Finally, call out, "Let the show begin!" _____ First, collect the tickets on the night of the big show. _____ Then when everyone is seated, dim the lights. _____ Help people find their seats in the audience.

_____

_____ Next, the piano music started. _____ Then two puppets, a clown, and a donkey sang to the music. _____ Finally, the curtain came down. _____ First, the curtain went up. _____ Everyone laughed and clapped when the donkey sang "Hee-Haw."

- **Purpose** in writing is the reason why something is written.
- One purpose is to tell about a thought or feeling.
    EXAMPLE: I thought I'd never stop laughing.
- Another purpose is to describe something.
    EXAMPLE: The bright red color of the bird shone through the waving branches of the trees.
- Another purpose is to give information.
    EXAMPLE: The science fair is today.
- Another purpose is to tell about something that is make-believe.
    EXAMPLE: The snowflakes talked to one another as they fell to the ground.

- **Write a sentence that tells how you feel about going to puppet shows.**

_____

- **Write a sentence that describes a puppet.**

_____

_____

- **Write a sentence that gives some information about a puppet show.**

_____

_____

- **Write the first sentence of a make-believe story that could be used for a puppet show.**

_____

_____

Here are some steps to follow in choosing a **topic**.
- Write a list of persons, things, or animals that interest you. Then circle the topic that especially interests you.

    EXAMPLES: clowns, (putting on a puppet show), tigers
- Divide the topic into smaller parts. Choose the one that you would like to write about.

    EXAMPLES: making a princess puppet, sending out invitations, practicing for the show

- **You are going to write a paragraph. Your purpose is to give someone information about how to make something. You need to choose a topic. Write a list of different things you can make.**

1. _____

2. _____

3. _____

4. _____

5. _____

6. _____

- **Circle the topic that especially interests you.**

- **Divide the topic you circled into smaller parts. Underline the one you would like to write about.**

1. _____   4. _____

2. _____   5. _____

3. _____   6. _____

- The purpose of some paragraphs is to give instructions.
- A **how-to paragraph** tells how to do something.
  EXAMPLE:

  ### How to Make a Soap-Bottle King Puppet

  It is not hard to make a soap-bottle king puppet. To begin, search through your house for materials to make your puppet. You will need to find a dishwashing soap bottle, scrap cloth, paper, and markers. First, make the puppet head by turning the bottle upside down. Draw a face and hair on the bottle with markers. Next, glue a paper crown above the face. Then glue a piece of scrap cloth around the middle of the bottle. Put your finger in the opening of the bottle, and say "Hello" to the king.

- **Write the topic sentence for the paragraph in the box.**

_____

- **Write four sentences that give details about the topic.**

_____

_____

_____

_____

_____

_____

- **Look at the topic you chose on page 73. Write a how-to paragraph about your topic. Use the model on page 74 to help you. Be sure to include a good topic sentence and the steps you would follow.**

- An **invitation** is a kind of letter. An invitation tells the following things: **who** will give the event, **what** kind of event it will be, **when** it will begin and end, and **where** it will take place.
- An invitation includes the address or telephone number of the sender.

EXAMPLE:

> 569 North Street
> Akron, Ohio 44305
> August 6, 20____

Dear Jesse,
    Please come to a puppet show on Saturday, August 20. It will be at Mary Baldwin's house, 22 Oak Avenue, from 3:00 to 4:00. See you then!

> Your neighbor,

Call 555-6340   Craig

- **Write an invitation to a party you would like to have.**

_____

_____

_____

_____

_____

_____

_____

_____

_____

_____

_____

- A **telephone message** tells:
  1. The **day** and **time** the message was received.
  2. The **name** of the person getting the message.
  3. The **name** of the person who called.
  4. The **phone number** of the person who called.
  5. The important **information** from the call.
  6. The **name** of the person who took the message.

EXAMPLE:

4/18/04
10:15 A.M.

Jay—

   Beth Bishop called and wants you to call her back at 555-3958. She needs to ask you how to make soap-bottle puppets for her play.

Megan

- **Read this part of a telephone call. Then write the message Henry might leave for Terry. Write today's date and time.**

HENRY: "Terry isn't home. I'll take a message for him."

NANCY: "Please tell him to call me back at 555-2749. I want him to get some cloth for the puppets we're making. Thanks. Good-bye."

(Date) _____

(Time) _____

(To) _____

(Message) _____

_____

(From) _____

- **Write each thought as a sentence.**

  1. putting the puppet on my hand

  _____

  2. making the puppet nod its head

  _____

  3. moving the puppet's mouth

  _____

- **Circle the topic sentence in the paragraph below. Then underline only the sentences that give details about the main idea.**

  A break between acts in a play is needed. It allows time for the crowd to get up and stretch. Sarah is a very good math student. It lets the people in the show get ready for the rest of the play. It also gives time to prepare for the next act.

- **Write numbers to show the correct order of the details for each set of directions below.**

  _____ Then let the popcorn pop.   _____ First, pour popcorn into a pan.   _____ Finally, serve it to the crowd.   _____ Next, put a lid on top of the pan.

  _____

  _____ Then mix the juice and water together.   _____ Finally, pour the juice into glasses.   _____ First, spoon frozen juice into a pitcher.   _____ Next, add cold water.

- **Write a sentence that tells how you feel about owning a pet.**

_____

- **Write a sentence that describes a pet you own or would like to own.**

_____

_____

- **Write a sentence that gives some information about how to care for a pet.**

_____

_____

- **Write the first sentence of a make-believe story about a magical pet.**

_____

- **Write an invitation to a picnic that your class is having.**

_____

_____

_____

_____

_____

_____

_____

_____

■ **Read this story.**

One day Sam was looking for something fun to do. Sam decided he would like to ask his friend Hoan to come over to play. Sam's mother said that he should call Hoan after lunch. Sam was so excited, thinking about all the fun they'd have together. Since it was such a nice day, they would be able to play outside. Sam decided to ask Hoan to bring his bike so that they could ride together.

■ **Pretend that Hoan is not home when Sam calls. Write a telephone message for Hoan. Write the important information from the call. Use the correct names, today's date, the time, and your phone number.**

- **Write an invitation to a show that your class might put on.**

_____

_____

_____

_____

_____

_____

_____

_____

- **Write a how-to paragraph telling how to get to your house. Write a topic sentence and supporting details. Use words such as first, next, and then to put the details in order.**

_____

_____

_____

_____

_____

_____

_____

_____

- **Directions** must be followed step-by-step.
- Sometimes maps help you to follow directions. They might show which way is north, south, east, and west by the letters N, S, E, and W.

  EXAMPLE:

Directions to Mary's House

1) Go north on Oak Street.
2) Turn east on Olive Avenue.
3) Walk down 3 houses to 56 Olive Avenue.

- **Look at the map, and read the directions to Joseph's house. Then answer the questions.**

1) Go south on Cook Street.
2) Turn west on Forest Road.
3) Walk down 6 houses to 846 Forest Road.

1. What direction should you go first? _____

2. What street should you walk on first? _____

3. What direction should you go next? _____

4. What street would you be on? _____

5. How many houses down Forest Road is Joseph's house? _____

- Carefully read everything before beginning to follow written directions.
- Pay close attention to words that tell the order of the steps you must follow.

  EXAMPLES: first, second, next, later, then, now, finally
- Be sure to follow the directions exactly as they are written.

- **Read the recipe shown below. Then answer the questions.**

Chocolate Banana Pops

First, remove the banana peel, and cut the banana into four pieces. Next, push a popsicle stick into the center of each piece. Then put the banana pops on a cookie sheet and freeze them. Melt $\frac{1}{2}$ cup (125 ml) chocolate chips and 2 tablespoons (30 ml) margarine over low heat. Dip the frozen bananas in the chocolate. Place the chocolate-covered bananas on a cookie sheet covered with waxed paper, and place them in the freezer.

1. What tools do you need for this recipe? _____

_____

2. What ingredients do you need? _____

_____

3. What should you do just before you freeze the banana pops for the first time? _____

_____

4. What is the last thing you do to complete the recipe? _____

_____

Grouping

> ■ Things that are alike in some way can be **grouped** together. The name of the group tells how the things in the group are alike.
> EXAMPLE: Dogs, cats, and horses are all animals.

■ **Underline the words that belong in each group.**

1. **animals**   sand   mouse   monkey   sheep   flower   bird

2. **foods**   bread   hat   egg   carrot   apple   fish

3. **colors**   blue   red   grass   purple   orange   cow

4. **fruits**   apple   cake   orange   milk   banana   grape

5. **clothes**   pants   foot   shirt   jacket   pale   hat

6. **round things**   ball   desk   circle   rake   penny   orange

7. **flying things**   bike   bird   jet   snake   rocket   turtle

8. **boys' names**   Peter   Ann   Mike   Jill   Josh   Tom

9. **girls' names**   Karen   David   Pam   Bill   Elaine   Melanie

10. **vegetables**   peas   apples   carrots   beans   corn   tuna

11. **tools**   hammer   saw   chair   shovel   rake   desk

■ **Write the words below under the correct heading.**

monkey	school	potato
carrot	elephant	store
house	corn	lion

Zoo Animals   **Vegetables**   **Buildings**

_____   _____   _____

_____   _____   _____

_____   _____   _____

■ The **table of contents** is in the front of a book. It lists titles and page numbers of parts of the book.

EXAMPLE:

Synonyms 1

Antonyms 2

Homonyms 3

More Homonyms 4

Words with More Than One Meaning 5

■ **Use the table of contents in this book to answer the questions.**

1. How many units are in this book? _____

2. What is the title of Unit 5? _____

3. On what page is "Using Commas in Sentences" in Unit 4? _____

4. What is the title of page 14? _____

5. On what page is "Writing Sentences" in Unit 5? _____

6. What is the title of page 48? _____

7. Which unit would help you learn more about grammar and usage?_____

8. On what page does Unit 6 begin? _____

9. On what page is "Compound Words" in Unit 1? _____

10. On what page does Unit 1 end? _____

11. On what page does the Unit 1 Final Review begin? _____

12. On what page does the Unit 5 Final Review end? _____

13. On what page is "Sentences" in Unit 2? _____

14. Which unit would help you learn more about vocabulary? _____

- An **index** is in the back of a book. It lists the subjects of the book in alphabetical order and gives page numbers.

  EXAMPLE:

  Abbreviations, 56, 57, 63, 66, 102, 103

  Adjectives

      definition of, 43

      identifying, 43, 44, 47, 51, 101

      that compare, 44, 49, 50, 101

      that describe, 43, 101

- **Use the index of this book to answer the questions.**

1. On what page is the index of this book? _____

2. What pages tell about suffixes? _____

3. What pages tell about antonyms? _____

4. What pages tell about quotation marks? _____

5. Are the words <u>business letters</u> listed in the index? _____

6. What pages tell about action verbs? _____

7. Under which heading should you look if you want to learn about homographs? _____

8. What are three examples of specific punctuation marks listed in the index? _____

9. Under which heading do you find letter writing? _____

10. What pages tell about telephone messages? _____

- **Alphabetical order** is the order of the letters in the alphabet. To put words in alphabetical order, look at the first letter of each word. Use the first letter of each word to put the words in the order of the alphabet.

  EXAMPLES: **b**ag, **p**ack, **c**ottage = **b**ag, **c**ottage, **p**ack

- Look at the second letter if the words begin with the same letter.

  EXAMPLES: **f**ish, **f**ry, **fe**ast = **fe**ast, **fi**sh, **fr**y

- **Write each set of words in alphabetical order.**

oar canoe paddle	giant good glass

1. _____
2. _____
3. _____

1. _____
2. _____
3. _____

town week ranch	bounce ball beach

1. _____
2. _____
3. _____

1. _____
2. _____
3. _____

east soap dream	pole price pump

1. _____
2. _____
3. _____

1. _____
2. _____
3. _____

- **Guide words** are at the top of each dictionary page. They show the first and last words on the page. Every word listed on the page comes between the guide words.
  EXAMPLE: **oak / real**

oak	*ɯɯɯɯ*
ocean	ready
ɯɯɯɯ	real

- **Write the pair of guide words that each word comes between.**

add / chase   quack / weep

1. beehive   _add / chase_   5. usual _____

2. reason _____ 6. cabin _____

3. wall _____ 7. quiet _____

4. attach _____ 8. spark _____

- **Write the word that would be on the same page as each set of guide words.**

iron	across	ill	dine	dad	job
arrow	weight	ship	wonder	herd	post

1. idea / in _____ 7. cut / desk _____

2. apple / ax _____ 8. serve / space _____

3. different / dry _____ 9. able / ago _____

4. jar / just _____ 10. wheat / wrong _____

5. insect / island _____ 11. hair / hose _____

6. wagon / winter _____ 12. pine / price _____

- Words that are listed on a dictionary page are called **entry words.** They are listed in alphabetical order.
- A dictionary gives the **definition,** or meaning, for each entry word.
- Some words have more than one meaning. Then each meaning is numbered.

  EXAMPLE:

  easy 1. not hard to do. **2.** free from trouble.

---

calf 1. a young cow or bull. **2.** the young of other animals.
call 1. to say in a loud voice. **2.** to give a name to. **3.** to make a telephone call.

carol a song.
carpet 1. a floor covering made of heavy cloth. **2.** to cover an area completely.

- **Read the definitions of each entry word. Then answer the questions.**

1. Which word has one meaning? _____

2. Which word has three meanings? _____

3. Which words have two meanings? _____

4. Which word means "a song"? _____

5. Write a sentence with one meaning of <u>carpet</u>. _____

_____

6. Write a sentence with one meaning of <u>call</u>. _____

_____

7. Write a sentence with the first meaning of <u>calf</u>. _____

_____

part 1. an amount less than the whole. 2. the line made when hair is combed. 3. an actor's role.
pass 1. to go by. 2. to do the opposite of fail.
peace 1. freedom from war. 2. quiet.
pen 1. something to write with. 2. a place to keep animals.

place 1. space taken up by a person or thing. 2. a city, town, country, or other area. 3. to put.
plant 1. a living thing that is not an animal. 2. to put something in the ground to grow.
point 1. a sharp end. 2. a method of scoring in a game. 3. the main idea or important part.

■ **The entry words in the box have more than one meaning. Write the number of the correct meaning next to each sentence.**

1. My old red pen ran out of ink. _____

2. Naomi couldn't find a place for her table. _____

3. They will plant daisies in the spring. _____

4. Arnold sat in the chair to get some peace. _____

5. Did most of the class pass the test? _____

6. Don't place the candles too near the heat. _____

7. What kind of plant are you growing? _____

8. The little pigs were in a pen. _____

9. Do you have to travel far to get to the place? _____

10. Did the car pass the truck? _____

11. Do the soldiers want peace or war? _____

12. Kirk scored ten points in basketball. _____

13. He only played for part of the game. _____

14. The teacher asks us to keep a point on our pencils. _____

15. Everyone had a part in our class play. _____

16. There was no part in her hair. _____

Dictionary: Pronunciation

> - Each word listed in a dictionary is followed by a respelling of the word. The respelling shows how to **pronounce,** or say, the word. The respelling is in parentheses following the entry word.
> - **Accent marks** show which word parts are said with the most force.   EXAMPLES: sər prīz′   tē′ chər
> - A **pronunciation key** (shown below) contains letters and special symbols, along with sample words, that show how the letters should be pronounced.

- **Use the pronunciation key to answer the following questions.**

1. What key word is given for u̇? _____

2. What key word is given for î? _____

3. What key words are given for ə? _____

_____

at; āpe; fär; câre; end; mē; it; īce; pîerce; hot; ōld; sông; fôrk; oil; out; up; ūse; rüle; pu̇ll; tûrn; chin; sing; shop; thin; <u>th</u>is; hw in white; zh in treasure. The symbol ə stands for the unstressed vowel sound in about, taken, pencil, lemon, and circus.

- **Study each respelling using the pronunciation key. Then circle the word that matches the respelling.**

1. (chōz)   shoes   chose   choice

2. (let′ûr)   letter   lettuce   ladder

3. (sī′əns)   since   scenes   science

4. (kär′tən)   cartoon   carton   garden

5. (<u>th</u>ēz)   these   this   those

6. (mezh′ûr)   messier   messenger   measure

7. (fü′əl)   fuel   full   file

■ **Read the directions below. Then answer the questions.**

> You can make a boat from half of a walnut shell. First, carefully open the shell by cracking it where the two halves join. Second, remove the nut from the shell. Then place one end of a toothpick into one end of a shell half. Next, glue the toothpick to the shell. Cut a small sail from construction paper. Finally, glue the sail to the toothpick.

1. What can you make using these directions? _____

_____

2. What should you do first? _____

_____

3. What should you do after you glue the toothpick to the shell? _____

_____

■ **Circle the words that belong in each group.**

1. **babies**   puppy   chick   cat   kitten   lamb   dog

2. **seasons**   fall   day   spring   summer   rain   winter

3. **fruit**   beans   apples   oranges   peas   pears   seeds

■ **Write the name of the group for each set of words.**

1. pants   dress   shirt   skirt   coat

_____

2. lunch   supper   breakfast   dinner

_____

3. red   green   yellow   blue   orange

- **Write each list of words in alphabetical order.**

1. seen _____
   lake _____
   cage _____

2. blue _____
   bee _____
   bat _____

3. press _____
   plow _____
   puff _____

- **Use the index in this book to answer the following questions.**

1. What page gives a definition of adverbs? _____

2. What pages tell about exclamation points? _____

3. What pages tell about homonyms? _____

- **Read the dictionary entries for <u>stalk</u> and <u>stand</u>. Write the meaning that goes with each sentence below.**

1. I watched the cat <u>stalk</u> the wind-up toy.
   _____

2. Let's <u>stand</u> up and stretch.
   _____

3. We put the <u>stalk</u> in water to keep the plant alive.
   _____

4. I can't <u>stand</u> the smell of onions.
   _____

> **stalk 1.** the stem of a plant. **2.** to hunt
> **stand 1.** to be on one's feet. **2.** to put up with.

- **Study each respelling using the pronunciation key. Then circle the word that matches the respelling.**

1. (ô′fŭl)   official   awful   useful

2. (rīm)   rhyme   rim   room

3. (van)   vane   van   than

> at; āpe; fär; câre; end; mē; it; īce; pîerce; hot; ōld, sông; fôrk; oil; out; up; ūse; rüle; pu̇ll; tûrn; chin; sing; shop; thin; <u>th</u>is; hw in white; zh in treasure. The symbol ə stands for the unstressed vowel sound in about, taken, pencil, lemon, and circus.

■ Imagine you are going shopping in a grocery store. To make your shopping trip quicker and easier, put the food items on the shopping list below into the groups in which they belong.

Shopping List: canned soup, potatoes, bananas, frozen orange juice, lettuce, chicken, broccoli, hamburger, apples, bacon

Fruits

_____

_____

_____

Canned

_____

_____

_____

Vegetables

_____

_____

_____

Frozen

_____

_____

_____

Meat

_____

_____

_____

■ Use the table of contents in this book to answer the following questions.

1. What is the title of page 25? _____

2. On what page is "Linking Verbs" in Unit 3? _____

3. On what page is "Guide Words" in Unit 6? _____

4. What is the title of the lesson on page 85? _____

5. How many pages are in Unit 1? _____

6. What is the title of Unit 2? _____

- **Follow the directions to Diane's house. Circle her house on the map.**

1. Go west on Peach Street.

2. Turn north on Bell Lane.

3. Go down 5 houses to 308 Bell Lane.

- **Write directions to 296 Bell Lane.**

_____

_____

_____

- **Draw a map showing the street where you live.
  Draw a line to show what street crosses yours.
  Then write the directions to where you live.**

_____

_____

_____

Synonyms and Antonyms ▪ Write S if the underlined words are synonyms. Write A if they are antonyms.

_____ 1. The driver couldn't see through the thick <u>fog</u> and <u>mist</u>.

_____ 2. The gas tank went from <u>full</u> to <u>empty</u> in minutes.

_____ 3. We couldn't see to our <u>right</u> or to our <u>left</u>.

_____ 4. We had to <u>stop</u> on the side and wait for help because our car just wouldn't <u>go</u> anymore.

_____ 5. When we stopped it was <u>light</u> outside, but now it is getting <u>dark</u>.

_____ 6. We thought it would be a <u>short</u> wait, but no one came for a <u>long</u> time.

Homonyms ▪ Circle the correct homonym to complete each sentence.

1. Shanelle has been invited (two, to, too) a party.

2. Denise is going to the party, (too, to, two).

3. She asks Denise if the party starts at (to, too, two) o'clock.

4. Denise tells Shanelle that she needs to be (there, their, they're) at four o'clock.

5. The girls can hardly wait to (here, hear) that it is time for the party.

6. They plan to meet (here, hear) and go together.

Words with More Than One Meaning ▪ Read the meanings in the box. Write the number of the meaning for each underlined word.

_____ **1.** Tony turned on the light so he could see.

_____ **2.** He picked up a light piece of wood.

_____ **3.** It weighed less than one pound.

_____ **4.** He used a special tool to pound a design into the wood.

> **pound** **1.** a weight equal to 16 ounces **2.** to hit hard over and over
> **light** **1.** not heavy **2.** something by which we see

Prefixes ▪ Underline the prefix. Write the meaning of the word.

1. unable _____

2. relive _____

3. repay _____

Suffixes ▪ Underline the suffix. Write the meaning of the word.

1. worker _____

2. dryer _____

3. visitor _____

Compound Words and Contractions ▪ Make a compound word or a contraction from each pair of words. Circle the contractions.

1. some + one = _____

2. she + is = _____

3. I + will = _____

4. day + light = _____

Types of Sentences ▪ Write <u>S</u> for statement, <u>Q</u> for question, <u>C</u> for <u>command</u>, or <u>E</u> for <u>exclamation</u> for each sentence. Write <u>X</u> if the group of words is not a sentence.

_____ **1.** Rob played basketball.

_____ **2.** How many points did Lee make?

_____ **3.** What a good player she is!

_____ **4.** Pass the ball to Lupe.

_____ **5.** Scored ten points.

_____ **6.** Which team do you think will win?

_____ **7.** I hope Pat's team wins.

_____ **8.** Both teams are doing a.

_____ **9.** Lupe bounced the ball to Rob.

_____ **10.** Shoot the ball, Rob.

Subjects and Predicates ▪ Underline each subject. Circle each predicate.

1. The new game began.

2. Jay quickly bounced the ball.

3. Vicki picked up the pass.

4. Todd blocked the shot.

5. Carl jumped for the ball.

6. The other team got the ball.

7. Lisa tried to shoot a basket.

8. The ball bounced off the rim.

9. Vicki scored two points.

10. Everyone gave a loud cheer.

Combining Subjects and Predicates ▪ Combine the sentences. Write the new sentences.

1. Dan signaled to Jack. Dan passed the ball.

   _____

2. Vincenté wanted to play. Tamara wanted to play.

   _____

3. They won today. They lost last week.

   _____
   _____

Writing Clear Sentences ▪ Read the sentences. Write two sentences for each.

1. Mark enjoys all kinds of sports, his favorite sport is basketball.

   _____
   _____

2. Mark's mother used to play basketball, she was on a team in high school.

   _____
   _____

3. Mark finds a photo of his mother playing basketball, he shows it to his friend Tina.

   _____
   _____

4. Tina's mother is in the photo, her mother used to play basketball, too.

   _____
   _____

Singular and Plural Nouns ▪ Write **S** before each
singular noun. Then write its plural form. Write **P**
before each plural noun. Then write its singular form.

_____ 1. inches _____   _____ 4. boxes _____

_____ 2. toe _____   _____ 5. cart _____

_____ 3. bus _____   _____ 6. tigers _____

Proper and Common Nouns ▪ Write **P** before each
proper noun. Then write a common noun for it.
Write **C** before each common noun. Then write a
proper noun for it.

_____ 1. friend _____   _____ 3. school _____

_____ 2. Texas _____   _____ 4. Lake Erie _____

Verbs ▪ Underline each action verb. Circle each
linking verb. Write **present** or **past**.

1. Katie lives in Chicago.   _____

2. I visited her in June.   _____

3. Diane was in Chicago last year.   _____

Using the Correct Verb ▪ Draw a line under the
correct verb.

1. Joel (saw, seen) the train pulling out of the station.

2. He needed to (buy, buys) a ticket to Chicago, Illinois.

3. Joel (runs, run) to catch the train.

4. He should (have, has) gotten there earlier.

5. Joel (were, was) waving to get the train to stop.

6. But the train (did, do) not stop.

Using the Correct Pronoun • Draw a line under the correct pronoun.

1. Nina's father gave (her, she) a new camera.

2. She wants to learn to take pictures with (them, it).

3. (She, Her) father will show her how the camera works.

4. Nina and (she, her) dad take some pictures.

5. Nathan and (I, me) are Nina's cousins.

6. We hope she sends (we, us) copies of the photos.

Adjectives • Underline each adjective.

1. Dinosaurs were once the largest reptiles on Earth.

2. Some dinosaurs ate green plants.

3. Other animals felt safer around dinosaurs that ate plants.

4. Some dinosaurs ate fresh meat.

5. It was dangerous for other animals to be close to one of these hungry dinosaurs.

Adverbs • Underline each adverb.

1. Dinosaurs lived happily for a long time.

2. Scientists have carefully studied how dinosaurs lived.

3. There are no dinosaurs alive today.

4. Scientists do not know exactly what happened to them.

5. They have worked very hard to find reasons why the dinosaurs died.

Capitalizing Proper Nouns • Rewrite the words.
Use capital letters where needed.

1. december _____
2. winter _____
3. monday _____
4. my sister _____
5. louise _____
6. new year's day _____

7. california _____
8. denver _____
9. thanksgiving _____
10. canada _____
11. tomás _____
12. store _____

Capitalization • Circle the letters that should be capitalized.

1. my family lives in orlando, florida.

2. i go to school at lincoln elementary.

3. mrs. n. kelly is my teacher this year.

4. my class has been studying dinosaurs.

5. she is taking us to a museum.

6. we'll get to see dinosaur bones at the museum.

7. the museum is north of our school.

8. it is on jones street near academy theater.

9. it is called the charles c. adler museum.

10. the museum is closed on sunday and monday.

11. we're going there on the first tuesday in march.

12. mr. peterson, our principal, says we will have a great time.

Punctuation ▪ **Put periods, commas, question marks, quotation marks, and apostrophes where needed.**

1. Mrs Kelly asked the people at the museum if they were ready for us

2. Yes they were ready for our class

3. We saw dinosaur bones snakes and birds at the museum

4. I didnt see all of the birds but I saw all of the dinosaurs bones

5. We watched a film about baby dinosaurs

6. Adam asked Have you ever seen a film about baby dinosaurs before

7. Hoan said No I havent

8. I liked the film the cave and the dinosaur footprints the best said Neal

9. Lets plan another trip for next month said Mrs Kelly

10. Do you think Mr Peterson will let the class come back

Parts of a Letter ▪ **Rewrite the parts of a letter. Use capital letters and commas where they are needed.**

1. dear zach _____

2. june 1 2004 _____

3. houston texas 77072 _____

4. sincerely _____

5. april 9 2005 _____

6. your friend _____

7. dear jesse _____

8. kansas city missouri 64114 _____

Writing Sentences ▪ Write each thought as a sentence.

1. watching television after dinner

_____

2. laughing at the funny lines

_____

3. eating popcorn as I watch

_____

Writing Paragraphs ▪ Circle the topic sentence in each paragraph. Then number the sentences in the correct order.

_____ Next, practice saying your part in front of a mirror. _____ The first thing you can do to make yourself feel better is to get used to being on a stage.

_____ Finally, ask some friends or family members if they will listen as you practice. _____ Most people get scared when they have to act in front of people.

_____ First, some students held imaginary cameras. _____ Yesterday Ms. Yamata's class put on a television show. _____ After the show was over, the class discussed what they had learned. _____ Then other students acted out a story.

Writing a How-to Paragraph ▪ Write a paragraph that tells how to make a peanut butter and jelly sandwich. Be sure to include a good topic sentence and the steps you would follow.

_____

_____

_____

_____

_____

_____

_____

Writing a Telephone Message ▪ Read what was said in this telephone call. Then write the message Claudia might leave for Tony. Write today's date and time.

CLAUDIA: "No, I'm sorry. Tony isn't home right now. May I take a message?"

KIM: "Yes, please tell him that he needs to call me at work. The number here is 555-9487. I need to ask him about a computer problem we are having. Thank you. Good-bye."

(Date) _____

(Time) _____

(To) _____

(Message) _____

_____

(From) _____

Following Written Directions ▪ Read the directions and study the map. Then answer the questions.

Go east past the high school.
Turn north on Oak Road.
Go three blocks until Oak Road ends.

1. Which direction do you go to pass the high school? _____

2. What is the name of the road on which you turn north? _____

3. To what building do these directions lead you? _____

Grouping ▪ Write the words from the box under the correct heading.

toast	spaghetti	pancakes
fish	popcorn	raisins

Breakfast   **Dinner**   **Snacks**

_____   _____   _____

_____   _____   _____

Using a Table of Contents and an Index ▪ Answer the following questions.

1. Where in a book would you find a table of contents? _____

2. What information does a table of contents list? _____

3. Where in a book would you find an index? _____

4. In what order are the subjects listed in an index? _____

Alphabetical Order ▪ Write each list of words in alphabetical order.

1. rake _____

   scare _____

   sat _____

2. teeth _____

   cause _____

   cheer _____

Guide Words ▪ Study the dictionary page on the right. Write the guide words for the page.

_____ / _____

| leather ᴧᴧ ᴧᴧᴧᴧ ᴧᴧᴧᴧ |
| ᴧᴧᴧᴧ ᴧᴧᴧᴧ ᴧᴧᴧᴧᴧᴧ |
| ᴧᴧᴧᴧᴧᴧᴧ ᴧ ᴧᴧᴧ ᴧᴧᴧᴧ |
| ᴧᴧᴧᴧ ᴧᴧᴧᴧ lie ᴧᴧᴧᴧ |

Words with More Than One Meaning ▪ Read the dictionary entry for <u>batter</u>. Write the number of the meaning that is used in each sentence.

_____ 1. James mixed the <u>batter</u> for two minutes.

_____ 2. The second <u>batter</u> hit a home run.

batter 1. a mixture of flour, milk, and eggs used in cooking. **2.** a player whose turn it is to bat.

Pronunciation ▪ Study each respelling using the pronunciation key. Then circle the word that matches each respelling.

1. (noi′ zē)   nose   notes   noisy

2. (drô′ ing)   growing   drawing   drowning

3. (sum′ ər)   summary   summer   simmer

4. (fus)   fuse   fuss   fish

5. (ə wâr′)   beware   aware   wear

6. (on′ ûr)   under   onward   honor

at; āpe; fär; câre; end; mē; it; īce; pîerce; hot; ōld; sông; fôrk; oil; out; up; ūse; rüle; pull; tûrn; chin; sing; shop; thin; this; hw in white; zh in treasure. The symbol ə stands for the unstressed vowel sound in about, taken, pencil, lemon, and circus.

Index